Are You a Newrotic?

A Guide to Fashionable Psychological Disorders

John Flowers and Bernard Schwartz
Illustrated by
Chan Lowe

Prentice-Hall, Inc., Englewood Cliffs, New Jersey 07632

Library of Congress Cataloging in Publication Data

Flowers, John V. (date).
 Are you a newrotic?

 1. Psychology, Pathological—Anecdotes, facetiae,
satire, etc. I. Schwartz, Bernard (date).
II. Title. III. Title: Are you a neurotic?
RC343.F615 1983   616.89'00207   83-17786
ISBN 0-13-045436-2
ISBN 0-13-045428-1 (pbk.)

© 1984 by John V. Flowers, Bernard Schwartz, and Chan Lowe.
All rights reserved. No part of this book may be reproduced in any form
or by any means without permission in writing from the publisher.
Printed in the United States of America.

10 9 8 7 6 5 4 3 2 1

Editorial/production supervision by Chris McMorrow
Cover design by Hal Siegel
Manufacturing buyer: Pat Mahoney

This book is available at a special discount when ordered in
bulk quantities. Contact Prentice-Hall, Inc., General
Publishing Division, Special Sales, Englewood Cliffs, N.J. 07632.

ISBN 0-13-045436-2
ISBN 0-13-045428-1 {PBK.}

PRENTICE-HALL INTERNATIONAL, INC., London
PRENTICE-HALL OF AUSTRALIA PTY. LIMITED, Sydney
PRENTICE-HALL CANADA INC., Toronto
PRENTICE-HALL OF INDIA PRIVATE LIMITED, New Delhi
PRENTICE-HALL OF JAPAN, INC., Tokyo
PRENTICE-HALL OF SOUTHEAST ASIA PTE. LTD., Singapore
WHITEHALL BOOKS LIMITED, Wellington, New Zeland
EDITORA PRENTICE-HALL DO BRASIL LTDA., Rio de Janeiro

Contents

Introduction vii

NEWROSES OF ADULT LIVING

Androgophobia 3
Psychophoria 6
Expectant Personality Disorder 9
Hebrewphrenia 12
Pretraumatic Stress Syndrome 15
Reverse Paranoia 19
Hypercondriacs 21
The Adequate Personality Disorder 22
Metaphilia 25
Vidiots 29
Walkmaniacs 31
Schizophonia 32
News-osis 34
Chronophiliacs 35
R-2 D-2 Personality Disorder 36

ROMANTIC AND SEXUAL NEWROSES

Incognitis Contrasexualis   41
Dubiophilia   42
Retrophilia   43
Manic Repression   45
Clitoral Envy   49
Inhibitionism   51
Postmature Ejaculation   53
Mammometricitus   55
Nymphomeloncholia   57
Soap Opera Personality Disorder   58
Noxiophilia   60

NEWROSES OF PARENTING

Childhood   65
Montessoria   69
Permissive Parent Burnout   70
Pedophobia   72
Retroactive Birth Control   74
Underanxious Child Syndrome   77

NEWROSES MAKERS

NEWroses-Producing Politicians 83
*NEWroses-Producing
Geographic Locations* 84
NEWroses-Producing Movies 85
*NEWroses-Producing Diet
and Exercise Programs* 86
Achievement Awards 87

Introduction

At a recent convention of WCPPSWAM (West Coast Psychologists, Psychiatrists, Social Workers, and Masseurs), a consensus was reached on one major issue: The old neuroses are out, and the NEWroses are in. Therapists report that they can no longer keep up with the new disorders from which their patients are suffering. The textbooks are outdated, the old treatments are not working, and even advice columnist Ann Landers is running old letters to avoid dealing with today's problems.

This book fulfills the need for a comprehensive analysis of the major emotional problems facing modern man and woman. Throughout history, from our humble beginnings as Peking Man, to today's Pac-Man, our species has had to continually adapt to new environmental stresses. Stresses can make you neurotic; modern stresses can make you NEWrotic. *Are You a NEWrotic?* will enable you to determine which contemporary maladies you might have—and will further advise you as to what you should or should not do about these problems. If you find, after perusing the book, that you aren't NEWrotic, and you feel left out, you can become a part of the avant-garde by simply emulating one of these fashionable and forward-looking psychological syndromes. After all, an Oedipus Complex might have been intriguing in Freud's day, but in today's competitive society, such a complaint would merely bore your spouse, friends, and therapist. It is our hope that this book will guide you in becoming as NEWrotic as you want.

I

NEW ROSES OF ADULT LIVING

It's not easy keeping it together in an age where the "Man of the Year" is a computer. The following NEW-roses show just how hard it really is.

Androgophobia

The fear of insulting a feminist and being labeled a male chauvinist.

In the beginning, man was boss. And he saw that it was good—and he was happy. But women were not. They wanted more than to make men happy. Men could not understand that. Women likened such men to a lowly barnyard animal. Men had their feelings hurt. They asked women why they had been forsaken. They tried to atone. Many went too far. They developed strange and debilitating behaviors. Shelter homes were established for the most severe cases.

We recommend that you alert yourself to the following symptoms:

1. You stammer when trying to pronounce Miss, Mrs., or Ms.
2. You are giving your daughter boxing lessons.
3. You are using your wife's last name instead of your own.

4. You say "personhole cover," "person-a-live," and "personhunt."

5. Your children have androgynous names such as North, Alpha, or Bagel.

ANDROGOPHOBIA
"It's Per-Per-Personischewitz Concord Grape . . . you like it?"

Treatment

If you are suffering from this disorder, you must stop feminism before it stops you.

- **A.** Use sign language when speaking to women.
- **B.** Insist that women call married men, Mr.; single men, Mirr.; and independent men, Msr. (stands for Master).
- **C.** Request that your local university start a program in Men's Studies. Courses should include "The Castrated Male" and "Great Males in the Secretarial and Nursing Fields."

Remember, unless you men arise and unite at this crucial point in history, don't be surprised when you find yourselves serving tea to your wives on Mondays as they watch Monday Night Sewing on T.V.

Psychophoria

A Case History

When he first arrived at the clinic, he described his prior therapy experiences: while in Gestalt Therapy, he had nearly gagged on an "aha" experience; in Transactional Analysis, he learned how to free his "child within" and is now having toilet accidents; and, after learning how to be "centered," he is able to stand only in the middle of rooms. He had endured Rolfing, Acupressure, and Bioenergetics without too much damage, but Polarity Therapy was more than he could take. Somehow in the course of treatment his poles were reversed. Consequently, when he came to therapy, in order for him to raise his right hand he had to think of raising his left foot instead. To brush his teeth it was necessary to think of putting on his socks.

This is a case history of a typical Psychophoric; one who suffers from the delusional belief that modern psychology can in some way help people.

Whereas early psychologists realized that the best their patients could hope for was to accept and adapt to unhappiness, contemporary head healers would have you believe that in regards to happiness, "the sky's the limit," and that you can "pull your own strings," "negotiate anything," and even raise a perfect dog "the Woodhouse way."

The truth of the matter is that: other people pull your strings—usually from opposing directions; you can't negotiate anything because everyone else believes in "winning through intimidation;" and "the limits of the sky are full of pie."

Treatment

If you have this disorder, a first step towards mental health is to avoid seeking professional help. Instead you should make use of aversive conditioning by connecting a feeling of nausea with the field of psychology. Begin by making yourself nauseous any way you can. (Reading a page of the *National Enquirer* or drinking a mixture of toothpaste and orange juice will do.) Next spend several minutes looking at pictures of Freud, Joyce Brothers, and Wayne Dyer. (Sometimes the pictures alone will induce nausea.) In a short while you will forever be rid of any interest in psychotherapy whatsoever. With luck, an appreciation of sociology and anthropology can be cured as well.

EXPECTANT PERSONALITY DISORDER
Expectant Reader.

Expectant Personality Disorder

A problem of those who expect more than this or any other world has to offer.

This is also known as "Inevitable Disappointment Syndrome." In times past, people did not expect much and were therefore rarely disappointed. Today we are told that nothing is out of our reach. In the best-seller *Life Extension,* men are told they can live forever without going bald. In *Nice Girls Do* women learn that a mere orgasm is an insult, and that they should strive instead for the "maxi-orgasm." We are all taught that "anyone in the U.S. can grow up and become president." In effect, we have come to "dream the impossible dream" as the following quotes demonstrate:

> **Expectant Teacher:** "Every child, given the right stimulation and patience, can achieve his potential."
>
> **Expectant Philosopher:** "I have it! I can prove I exist, I think."

Expectant Clergyman: "I have it! I can prove God exists, I think."

Expectant Husband: "A good wife is trustworthy, loyal, helpful, friendly, courteous, kind, *obedient,* cheerful, thrifty, brave, clean, and reverent."

Expectant Wife: "Someday he'll change."

Expectant Child: "My parents will treat me different when I am older."

Expectant Politician: "You can keep your integrity and still win an election."

Expectant Humorist: "Surely someone will laugh at this."

Treatment

If you frequently find that your reach exceeds your grasp, we recommend that you apply "Cognitive Mutilation Therapy."

Begin by copying the immortal words of Vince Lombardi on his philosophy of winning: "Winning isn't everything, it's the only thing." Each day read this sentence backwards one hundred times until you have no idea at all what winning is. Secondly, wear rubber bands around your wrists at all times. Whenever you use the word "goal" in a sentence pull the rubber band as far back as you can and let go. Try to muffle your screams. Finally, read the data published by the U.S. Census Department on the life-span of high-achievers and be happy with your attainment of mediocrity.

In the old days, before twenty-four hour news stations, people had a limited number of things about which to worry. Today the possibilities are limitless, creating the following NEWrosis.

Hebrewphrenia

People with this disorder (not necessarily Jewish) worry about almost everything—their children, pollution, population growth, getting enough fiber in their diet—you name it. Because they are so busy worrying, Hebrewphrenics are late to almost every engagement while worrying constantly about their lateness. In that rare moment when a Hebrewphrenic is not worrying, he focuses entirely on feeling guilty for the sins that he, his children, and his ancestors may have committed.

Are You a Hebrewphrenic?

1. Where are your keys, wallet, and appointment book right now?
2. If you have an appointment at three-thirty and it takes half an hour to get there, at what time should you leave to get there on time?
3. You have only enough money for an operation on your gall bladder or a better car for your wife. What do you do?
4. What did your mother say to you at every meal?

Answers

1. You should be clutching them at all times.
2. Three-thirty.
3. Ask wife permission to buy the car next year.
4. Eat everything on your plate. Think of all the children starving in China (India, Mexico, Africa, Appalachia).

Treatment

If this describes you, you have to find a very special type of wife—one who will continuously make impossible demands on you. Such a spouse (commonly referred to as a Jewish American Princess) has often been maligned for her unreasonable expectations. In reality, hers is an act of self-sacrifice that will keep you continually focused on your every failing in the marriage, leaving you no time to worry about anything else.

Pretraumatic Stress Syndrome

Those who suffer from this disorder are certain that since nothing traumatic has ever happened to them, something is bound to happen soon.

Never before in history have so many had it so good. And that's exactly what worries those with Pretraumatic Stress Syndrome.

Seek help immediately for this problem if you: routinely phone hospitals to see if family members have been injured; read the Sunday want ads to prepare for the possibility of being fired (even though you own your own company); use every spare dollar to buy more car, house, disability, life, or pet insurance.

TREATMENT FOR PRE-TRAUMATIC STRESS SYNDROME
"Come see Junior's Halloween costume . . . he made it all by himself."

Treatment

The only known cure for this disorder is to get the trauma over with. Drive by mental hospitals and pick up hitchhikers; move to Three Mile Island; arm your spouse with a pistol before confessing that you've been faking your orgasms for years, and that you have put up one of the kids for adoption.

A little creativity can pay off with great benefits and you can get on with a "normal" life of complaining about the awful things that have really happened.

As 1984 approached, people became more and more paranoid until some folks went over the edge and developed the following NEWroses.

Reverse Paranoia

Reverse Paranoids suffer from the belief that they are following somebody. In the more severe condition Reverse Paranoids believe they are persecuting someone; and in advanced stages they believe they can read other people's minds. (It may occur that the person being followed by the Reverse Paranoid remains stationary for an extended period of time. In such cases, the Reverse Paranoid is often mis-diagnosed as "Catatonic.")

In the United States there are more people following others than there are people to follow. Hence, many Reverse Paranoids have had to double up while trailing their victim. This has greatly increased the rate of traditional paranoia in this country.

Treatment

If you suspect that you are a Reverse Paranoid, clip out the following paragraph, place it in your wallet or purse, and read it before meals:

"I am following other people because they have tricked me into doing so. I am persecuting other people because other people want me to persecute them for all of the evil things that they have done. Thus other people must be controlling me in order to get me to follow and persecute them."

This unique approach, called "Cancellation Therapy", works by forcing patients to develop symptomatologies which are the exact opposite of their current problem. One hopes that when the dust settles there is nothing left (of the pathology). If you find after treatment that you have turned into a full-blown paranoid, this is because you are also a Psychophoric, one who takes psychological advice too seriously.

Another approach, "Sacrificial Therapy" requires the reverse paranoid to follow those suffering from Inverse Paranoia—the condition of those who feel they are not good enough to be followed or persecuted by anyone. This cures the Inverse Paranoid, and at least the Reverse Paranoid is no worse off.

Hypercondriacs

These are people who have followed every diet and exercise fad and are now so healthy that they fear they will never get sick enough to take a day off from work. People with extreme cases are afraid that they will live forever.

The Adequate Personality Disorder

Found in those who exhibit unusually high levels of contentment and self-regard.

Are you currently involved in a romantic relationship that has lasted more than three months?

Do you know the difference between an IRA, the IRS, and the PLO?

Do you know your driver's license number, zip code, and automatic bank teller security number by heart?

Is your resting pulse less than sixty-five beats per minute?

If you answered affirmatively to any of these questions, then you are showing definite signs of being adequate. Whereas at one time such strength of character would have been applauded, in today's highly unstable world where few can cope, stability can only lead to an intense feeling of alienation and guilt as the following case history demonstrates:

"You've got to help me doctor," the patient implored. "What is wrong with me? Why aren't I insecure, incompetent, and incomplete like all my friends? I feel so alone. And when they call me day and night with endless stories of their personal failings, gripes, and suffering, it makes me feel so guilty. I just want to be normal like everyone else."

Such is the plight of the adequate person in today's world.

Treatment

If you are among the oppressed minority suffering from this disorder, you must first stop thinking like an adequate person. No longer are you to guide your life by such maxims as: "Think before you act;" "Learn to take the good with the bad;" and "Don't make mountains out of molehills." Instead, take the following steps.

1. Throughout the day, refuse to think before you act. If you catch yourself doing so, immediately act, and then think about it later.
2. Repeat the following sentence three times upon arising: "Taking the good with the bad would be fine if there was enough good, but unfortunately, there isn't."

3. Don't just make mountains out of molehills, create entire ranges. For example, when you have a simple cold, visualize yourself developing pneumonia; when your boss doesn't say hello to you one morning, imagine either that you'll soon be fired or that you are going deaf.

Remember that you *are* what you think (unless you don't think so, in which case you are not) and that "thinking inadequately" can be fun, gets people off your back, and enables you to start complaining like everyone else that life is unfair, that you can't cope, and that you don't have what it takes.

Metaphilia

A Case History

Born too late to march against the war in Vietnam, the patient vainly searched for causes to demonstrate against. In desperation he joined a "Bored-Again" religious group but left that when he heard about a sect in India that chanted naughty words while practicing Tantric Yoga. To his surprise he discovered that he didn't care for sex that much when there was no seduction involved. He currently teaches the Jane Fonda Workout to leaders of the nuclear disarmament movement.

Does this sound anything like you? If so you are a *Metaphiliac,* one who relentlessly searches for meaning, more meaning unfortunately than exists.

In the past, people had little time to search for much more than their next meal. Today, the quest for meaning has become a full-time occupation for many people who join dozens of social movements in their pursuit of fulfillment.

To test your Metaphiliac tendencies, see if you can correctly identify the following cause-oriented organizations from their descriptions.

1. The organization of pea farmers who promote their product on radio and television.
2. The group dedicated to finding the cure for the common cold.
3. Sister organization of T. H. E. N.
4. People who give you flowers at airports.

Answers:

1. Greenpeace
2. Common Cause
3. N. O. W.
4. Unemployed members of the Screen Actors Guild

You probably won't admit to having this disorder if you are feeling "connected" at the present time. However, if you are feeling depressed and this description fits you, then the solution is for you to become an "Anti-cause Crusader."

Some tips are:

1. Campaign for James Watt for president of the Sierra Club.
2. Complain to the Public Broadcasting System about the lack of sex and violence on Sesame Street.
3. Pretend to circulate voter petitions but simply fill in the names from rosters of professional baseball and football teams.
4. Print up bumper stickers which state, "One nuclear bomb could make another Grand Canyon."

The "Anticause Crusade," unlike other movements that come and go, will endure because uncured Metaphiliacs will provide a never-ending source of "meanings" worthy of debunking.

Whereas the preceding NEWroses are all related to changing societal values and lifestyles, there is another class of disorder caused by technological and scientific advances. At this time, there are no cures for these problems. In fact, most NEWrotics who suffer from these conditions do not think there is anything wrong with themselves. Many do not think at all.

Television has affected all of our lives. However, for some, it has replaced living.

Vidiots

At first glance, these people seem normal enough as they sit before their television sets. However, soon the pattern emerges. Fused to their body, it seems, is a remote control box the size of a typewriter keyboard. Every fifteen seconds or so they touch a button and the channel changes. You are exposed, in rapid succession, to a badminton tournament on an all-sports station, a Jerry Falwell look-a-like on KGOD, and the House of Representatives in session, with instant replays of close votes.

You inquire if there is a particular channel the Vidiot is trying to find. "No," he states, "It's much more informative this way, and you never get bored." Changing the subject, you ask how things have been going. You are then given the latest stock quotations, the scores of Jai Alai games in Barcelona, and the weather out-look for the next century. "And the wife and kids?" you ask. "Oh we're all very busy, what with each of us having our own complete home entertainment center in our rooms, so we haven't seen much of each other lately. I do have a nice video of the family which I can show you on the Betamax machine...."

The effect of evolution on future generations of Walkmaniacs.

Walkmaniacs

These NEWrotics are noted for their almost continuous wearing of tiny headphones. They are distinguished by their ability to perform only limited human activities, their primary behavior pattern entailing rhythmic bouncing of the head while pretending to play imaginary musical instruments such as guitars and drums. Groups of Walkmaniacs have been sighted traveling on rollerskates and in cars, proof of the fact that they can be highly social. But only with repeated badgering and great reluctance will they remove their headphones so they can communicate verbally.

In view of the Walkmaniacs' antisocial behavior and unproductive lifestyle, leading geneticists fear that breeding with them will lead to mutations that could spell the end of the human race as we know it.

Schizophonia

The invention of the telephone allowed people to "reach out and touch someone" more conveniently than ever before in history. However, the telephone also gave birth to "Schizophonia," the fear of missing an important call by being too far from the phone.
    Early Schizophoniacs worked around this problem by purchasing longer extension cords, and installing phones in their basements, garages, and bathrooms. By applying such measures, the Schizophoniac was no longer confined to a single room. However, he was still too terrified to leave the house.
    The invention of the telephone answering machine seemed to be a miracle cure for this disorder. "Finally," the ads said, "you can be anywhere in the world and simply call your machine to pick up your messages." But alas, many people refused to speak to

answering machines and the only messages recorded were the sounds of dial tones as people hung up.

But the Schizophoniacs were not through yet. They began to devote all of their spare time and brainpower to producing creative recorded messages that were so entertaining, you wouldn't dream of hanging up without leaving your name and number at the beep. However, for some, the pressure to regularly produce new material was too much. They quit their jobs to work full time on their art. When they had used up their life's savings and could no longer afford to pay their bills, many were forced into taking up residence in telephone booths.

News-osis

This condition occurs in those who have seen one too many "live mini-cam reports" of floods, volcanic eruptions, hurricanes, tidal waves, and earthquakes, causing them to live in dire fear that a major disaster is headed in their direction.

Because of their anxiety, News-otics constantly search the world for a haven safe from the likelihood of a natural catastrophe. In order to avoid possible drowning, they refuse to live near rivers, lakes, oceans, or cesspools; cities along fault lines are definitely out; mountainous areas are excluded because they are susceptible to avalanches, and the tropics are vulnerable to monsoons and tourist inundation.

After much careful research, many News-otics banded together to settle in an unknown tiny community safe from all environmental assault, "Three Mile Island."

Chronophiliacs

These people are only happy when looking at and playing with their digital timepieces. If pressed once, these devices give you the local time; pressed twice, you're told the time in London; pressed a third time, and John Cameron Swayze tells you exactly how long you've owned your watch. Athletically-minded Chronophiliacs own watches which compute how long they've been jogging in tenths of seconds and also measure their pulses, their brain wave patterns, and the amount of tread left on their running shoes.

Some people hate the passage of time, want nothing to do with it, and have rebelled against measuring their lives on a minute-to-minute basis. These are the Chronophobics. In their entire lives, they have never owned a watch unless it was a gift, in which case it was given away immediately. They always forget important engagements because they refuse to invest in an appointment book, and they are forever late to work because they hate alarm clocks.

Chronophiliacs and Chronophobics can never, of course, relate successfully to one another. However, for some unexplained reason these people frequently join together in marriage, even though the Chronophobic is usually late for the wedding.

R-2-D-2 Personality Disorder

Those afflicted with this problem begin more and more to resemble their home computers until they seem devoid of all emotion, speaking in a continuous monotone with every word repeated at one second intervals. When they are willing to have you speak to them, which is rare, they state: "Ready to receive." If they can't understand you, which happens frequently, you are told: "Cannot Program."

R-2-D-2s spend every spare dollar to upgrade their units with special attachments, printers, and various software programs, including those which teach them foreign languages they will never speak because they rarely speak to people at all except in BASIC or PASCAL.

R-2 D-2 PERSONALITY DISORDER
"Hey, Baby, I really dig your software—care to come upstairs and check out some of my printed circuitry?"

Some of those suffering from this problem develop unnatural attachments to their floppy discs and treat them with the special care usually reserved for a loved one. In severe cases, several R-2-D-2s have been seriously injured when they tried to respond sexually to the computer instruction "Enter Input Now."

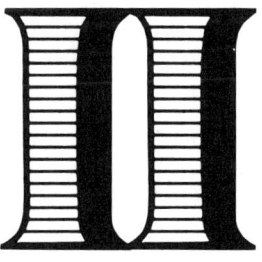

ROMANTIC AND SEXUAL NEUROSES

Eighty years ago Sigmund Freud asked the question: "What do women want?" Unfortunately, many social scientists took the question seriously and ever since have been steadfastly compiling data on both men and women in hopes of solving the mystery of the sexes once and for all. And after all of these years, what do we know?

Some of the major finds include:

> Women are usually shorter than men.
>
> Girls speak earlier than boys and males never fully catch up.
>
> Men are more aggressive than women except when women are mad.
>
> Boys usually masturbate more frequently, girls enter puberty earlier, and as far as we know, these two facts are not related.

In spite of the accumulation of this impressive storehouse of knowledge, it seems that men and women are as displeased with one another as ever. Whereas in previous generations couples worked around the problem, today's men and women make matters worse by working *on* the problem. The following NEWroses demonstrate the futility of such an approach.

Incognitis Contrasexualis

A condition in which, against all evidence and logic, people insist on trying to understand, please, and communicate with the opposite sex. This disturbance is caused by the absurd notion that both sexes are members of the same species and that they evolved on the same planet.

Dubiophilia

A disorder in which a couple is incapable of talking to one another about anything except their relationship.

Topics typically include:

1. Should we break up?
2. Should we see a counselor?
3. Should we date other people?
4. Do we expect too much of one another?
5. Are we ready for a serious relationship?

Usually, when the couple cannot decide on the answers to any of these questions, they then decide that it would be best to get married.

Retrophilia

The Liz and Richard Burton Syndrome

Retrophilia is a condition wherein the man and woman involved are not sure whether they are more miserable:

- **a.** in the relationship;
- **b.** in another relationship;
- **c.** in no relationship at all.

A true Retrophiliac examines each condition several times, creating more Retrophiliacs along the way.

MANIC REPRESSION
"Why, Dear, you haven't belched at me that way since the day we were married."

Manic Repression

The condition of believing that the inner core of one's mate is actually warm and exciting, but for some reason is now repressed and nonfunctional.

Almost from birth we are taught that the ultimate purpose of life is to meet and fall in love with a member of the opposite sex. At school, Dick and Jane no longer watch Spot run, they discuss contraception. On T.V., it's "Love Boat," "Love Story," and the "Love Canal." Later, we are taught that through love we will find fulfillment, learn selflessness, and reduce our income taxes.

Finding a person to do all of this for us is not easy. After years of fruitless searching, some people compromise their ideals; others give up the hunt entirely. However, Manic Repressives cannot handle the disappointment, and in desperation delude themselves into thinking they have found MR. or MRS. Perfect, when in reality they have found MR. or MRS. Average. After rushing into marriage, they then spend most of their energy trying valiantly to bring out the deep and interesting side of their spouse, continually failing since this side never existed.

Treatment

If this sounds like you, take a hard look at your mate and come to grips with exactly whom you *chose* to marry. While doing this you should take an antidepressant medication to help you through the trauma of this eye-opening experience.

The following questions will be useful in helping you to see your spouse more clearly (your real spouse, not the one you keep hoping to turn him into).

Mark true or false next to each statement:

1. My spouse mainly speaks to me in one and two word statements such as: "hum," "uh-huh," "oh," "I see," etc.
2. My spouse's idea of a vacation is watching Lawrence Welk reruns on a resort hotel television.
3. When I ask my spouse to share his feelings, he either makes a grab for my body or looks confused by the question.
4. The most exciting thing that happens on weekends is an oil change.
5. When I say "A penny for your thoughts," he says, "Keep your money, I don't want to cheat you."

Now that you know what you're coping with, apply a new relationship approach called "Digging Therapy." Get a shovel and visit various neighborhoods around your city and dig a hole at each site. Then inspect the dirt from each and keep notes on what you find. Nine times out of ten you will find the same old dirt. This experience should keep you from probing for the dark, mysterious, and nonexistent side of your spouse for quite some time.

One would have thought that with the advent of Masters and Johnson, the "Joy of Sex," and pastel prophylactics, sexual maladies would be a thing of the past. Instead, a whole new set of disorders, reflective of the times, has arisen.

Clitoral Envy

Exhibited by males who are jealous of the sexual superiority of women as evidenced by the female's ability to have multiple orgasms.

Men used to feed their egos by imagining that women were jealous of the male sexual apparatus. Many erected numerous phallic monuments to remind women of their inferiority. However, with the advent of "maxi-orgasms" men have now had to accept the fact that they are inferior to women sexually as well as biologically. This has caused a NEWrosis of dramatic proportions.

It is likely that you have clitoral envy if you:

1. Are a man.

Treatment

1. Homosexuality. This approach doesn't actually cure the envy, but at least you won't be continuously reminded of your sexual limitations.

2. Celibacy. Remember that the greatest religions of the world have struggled with the problem of Clitoral Envy longer than have psychologists. Refusing to play when you know you are second best can be a spiritual experience.

3. Negotiate a "good faith" contract with your wife. Under the terms of the contract she will limit her orgasms to a one-to-one ratio in exchange for terms such as: a bigger house, a new car of her choice (every year), a separate bank account, not having to visit her in-laws.

4. If all else fails, try a sex-change operation.

Inhibitionism

*A disorder afflicting those who are
ashamed of exhibiting
not only their private parts,
but also their public parts.
At its worst, they won't even exhibit
their private parts in private.*

Inhibitionism results when people have given up trying to compete with the perfect bodies displayed in magazines, television and movies. At first, many inhibitionists tried to bring their bodies up to the national standard through Beverly Hills, New York, and Scarsdale diets. For the most part, all they got was a severe state of geographic disorientation. Then they turned to physical regimens. They jogged, they swam, they aerobicized, they sang along with Richard Simmons, they threw themselves into Nautilus programs—they threw their backs out. They still didn't look like Brooke Shields or Tom Selleck, and they gave up. Now they won't look at themselves and they won't let anybody else look at them either.

Treatment

Don't worry—though the modern world caused this problem, modern science can cure it "one step at a time."

1. Have a life-size blow-up made of your favorite movie idol. (Choose a star of the same sex.)
2. Have a life-size blow-up made of yourself in which you are not wearing clothes.
3. Cut out your body parts from the photograph and put them in a pile.
4. Replace your idol's face with your own. Observe for ten minutes.
5. Continue this procedure everyday until you have replaced each of your idol's body parts with one of your own.

Isn't science wonderful?

Postmature Ejaculation

Afflicts those people who have read too many sex manuals that stress pleasing one's partner, with the result that they cannot have an orgasm before their mate does. This is not a problem until they meet another person suffering from the same disorder.

MAMMOMETRICITUS
"I don't know. He's been standing there like that for two and a half hours."

Mammometricitus

The disorder of those so concerned with breast size that it seems as though they think that intelligence, personality, and the soul are stored there.

Breasts have always had a special place in the hearts and minds of men. Recently, women like Marilyn Monroe and Dolly Parton have turned the breast into a national fixation.

Those with this problem commonly exhibit the following tendencies: They:

1. Get excited by balloons.
2. Store bowls upside down in their dish cabinet.
3. Get excited at numbers above thirty-six.
4. Buy 44D "training" bras for their lovers.

Treatment

If you have this disorder, the satiation cure is recommended. This involves joining the "LaLeche League" (National Order of Breastfeeders) and attending their international convention. Following this you will either have had your fill of breasts and be cured, or you will only be interested in dating women who are lactating.

Nymphomeloncholia

Created by the "Sexual Revolution," this disorder is characterized by extreme sadness resulting from one's inability to find a nymphomaniac.

Soap Opera Personality Disorder

This is a condition in which people do not feel truly alive unless:

- **A.** They think they are being jilted.
- **B.** They *are* being jilted.
- **C.** They are the one doing the jilting.

Historically, marriages were arranged by a trained expert who without the aid of computers matched couples on sensible bases such as wealth, title, and physical stamina. Today, without such guidance, the following NEWrosis has become a common pattern.

Noxiophilia

*The condition of being attracted
only to those with whom
one has nothing in common
(other than this disorder).*

A Case History

The case of any Noxiophiliac reads like a romance novel, without the happy ending.

Sally had been in love with John for eight years. For the first two years he had been married to someone else. For the next six he didn't want to rush into anything. Sally was a happy extrovert, John a critical introvert; Sally loved to party, John loved to work; Sally was Roman Catholic, John was Christian Scientist; Sally loved children, John hated them; Sally's friends didn't like John, John's friends despised Sally; Sally was monogamous, John was polygamous (but at least he was honest about it). When Sally's parents had tactfully tried to tell her that just maybe this wasn't the right man for her, she ceased visiting them. Sally's brothers and sister had given her similar advice and thus they also became *personae non gratae*. Sally, a very social person, sought new friends who might like John, and found none. Sally was unhappy and didn't understand why, for after all she was in love.

Treatment

Psychology can never alter the fact that opposites attract, but by studying the qualities that make for successful matches a Noxiophiliac can learn to resist succumbing to the fatal attraction.

Find the correct match for Sybil from the list on the right.

Sybil wants kids but not marriage

1. Phil is lonely and has a vasectomy
2. Jim is a priest
3. Bob wants to donate to a sperm bank
4. Janet had a sex change operation

If you are a Noxiophiliac, then you no doubt chose Phil or Janet. However, the correct match is Bob. Study this answer carefully until you get the idea. (If you're still confused, ask a happily married friend to explain the answer to you.) Now, from the same list, try to find the correct match for Beth who wants marriage but not children.

Under no circumstances are you to ever date again if you chose Jim as the correct match.

NEW ROSES OF PARENTING

You've read Dr. Spock? You watch Mr. Rogers religiously? You still can't understand your children and you want to run away from home? You are not alone as the following "NEWroses of Parenting" demonstrate.

Childhood

*The most common disorder of
parenting, caused by pregnancy,
requiring one to raise a person
who is
impossible to reason with,
impervious to discipline,
and prone to having far too much fun.*

Whereas, in the past, childhood was over in a flash, today it is not uncommon to hear of thirty-year-olds who are seriously thinking of moving out of their parents' home and getting a full-time job.

There is little one can do about "childhood" except to make sure that it ends as soon as possible. Therefore, in order to make sure your child gets the message that he is a short-term boarder, apply the following approaches.

Dealing with Childhood.

"Experience Broadening"

1. At a very early age get the children accustomed to spending large amounts of time in your neighbors' homes. Agree with your children when they tell you how much nicer they are treated by other parents.
2. Emphasize athletics so that you can send them to every sports camp imaginable.
3. Encourage your children to explore their family "roots" by shipping them off to relatives near, far, farther, and farthest.

"Individuation"

This approach entails moving the children to the farthest bedroom; then to the guest house, boarding school, Europe, and finally to the NASA space program.

"Aging Therapy"

In this method children are continually told to "grow up."

Lastly, in case your child should ever threaten to run away, always have a fully packed suitcase ready, containing winter and summer clothing, road maps, a compass, and passport.

MONTESSORIA
"Computer technology is just too hard to explain to a novice. Look—here's a Pac-Man cartridge. Why don't you go and play by yourself for a while."

Montessoria

The disorder wherein a child is smarter than either parent and grows more so each day.

---

1. Did you stop smoking and drinking when you were pregnant?
2. Did you have a natural childbirth?
3. Did you enroll your child in infant stimulation pre-schools, "mommy and me" swim programs, Scouts, Future Farmers of America, etc.?
4. Did you let your child beat you at games to help them gain self-confidence?
5. Did you answer rationally when your child asked you why they had to do something they didn't want to?

And now you complain that your child has an I.Q. twice your own?

AS YE SOW, SO SHALL YE REAP

Permissive Parent Burnout

Occurs in those who think their parents were tyrants, and who therefore wish to raise their children differently.

Case History

I swore I would never treat my children the way my parents treated me. So I prepared myself. I read all of the new child-rearing books: "Discipline Can Be Fun"; "The Children's Liberation Movement Handbook"; and "Toilet Training Your Teenager." I did everything the books told me. If my kids misbehaved, I never spanked them or stood them in the corner—I shared my feelings with them: "It worries me when you set the drapes on fire." "I'm concerned that you've been gone for a week without calling home." I never told them "because I said so" when they asked why they had to do something. Instead I explained things to them. Like when my son was poking his little sister in the eye, I said: "Eyes are very sensitive and when you do that it hurts." He poked her in the other eye.

Finally things got so bad I went to a psychologist. He told me to ignore the children when they misbehaved and to praise them if they behaved appropriately. Now the county social worker has accused me of neglect.

Recently some authority on nutrition was interviewed on a talk show and he said that kids act crazy when you feed them too much sugar-coated cereal; so I switched to honey. They poured a jar of it on the dog.

Right now I'm building a woodshed.

Treatment

Apply large amounts of a nearly forgotten approach to child-rearing—common sense.

Pedophobia

The fear of children (including neonates, infants, toddlers, pre-schoolers, early, middle, and late adolescents).

Pedophobia is technically an incorrect label for this disorder. Phobias are irrational fears, whereas this fear is totally rational, justified, and reasonable.

There's a good chance that you're a Pedophobic if you:

1. have ever turned off all the lights and pretended not to be home on Halloween night;
2. refuse to live in a neighborhood which is less than five miles from a college, ten miles from a high school, fifteen miles from an elementary school, and 100 miles from a pre-school;
3. avoid shopping centers which have hobby shops, video arcades, or ice rinks;
4. have an irrational desire to shoot your television set when Saturday morning cartoons come on.

Treatment

1. Begin by going to hospitals and looking at new-born infants. Stay behind the glass windows at all times. This will protect you as well as the babies.
2. Next, find an infant and actually touch it. Keep doing this for as long as possible, then rest and start again. A stiff drink may help in the beginning.
3. Next expose yourself to ever more dangerous age groups. Visit pre-schools during finger-painting and potty times, lead Cub Scout or Brownie groups on their first overnight hike, coach co-ed soccer teams.
4. Attend rock concerts of groups whose names sound like armed combat battalions (The Clash, X, Uriah Heep, Slash, etc.).

If the treatment is successful you may decide to become a parent, which creates an entire series of new disorders.

Retroactive Birth Control

The "idée fixe" in which a parent begins to obsessively fantasize having used birth control nine months prior to a child's birth.

Have you ever had the following thought, common to so many parents today: "Wouldn't it have been nice if we had put off having children for a little longer?" This is the earliest stage of the disorder. If you are not careful, within a short time it can progress to a wish, a want, a need, a hunger, a quest, and a crusade for pre-pregnant status. For some couples suffering from this syndrome, the only happy time during the month is the "menstruation celebration." On the other hand, children's birthdays can often precipitate severe panic reactions.

Treatment

If you have this malady, practice the following exercise at least once a day: Fantasize that your children have grown up, married, and become parents. As the fantasy proceeds you are to visualize that your grandchildren have complete control of the household and have imprisoned their parents in the bedroom. The grandchildren will only release their parents if a list of demands is met including a four-day school week and a cost-of-living increase in their allowance. While practicing the fantasy, you should repeat the following affirmation: "I only hope that when you have children, they do to you what you've done to me."

Every Saturday morning millions of children watch their favorite cartoon characters get beaten, kicked, dropped from planes, set on fire, and shot from cannons. Magically these same characters reappear the next week completely well and ready for more punishment. Is it any wonder that the following NEWrosis commonly plagues the modern parent?

Underanxious Child Syndrome

Underanxious children are those who are inappropriately courageous and take risks that petrify their parents. (This disorder causes a secondary disorder, Timidus Parentitis, wherein parents tremble a great deal of the time.)

UNDERANXIOUS CHILD SYNDROME
"I'm just going up to the roof for a second, Ma!"

The underanxious child:

1. Is not afraid of strangers and, in fact, frequently brings them home.
2. Will take candy and spaceship rides offered by interplanetary visitors.
3. Does not learn to swim by being *thrown* in the deep end: He or she jumps in.
4. Can destroy a neighborhood with a certified, non-explosive chemistry set.
5. Will broaden your education by introducing you to all of the doctors in your vicinity.
6. Will want a motorcycle as soon as he recovers from the injuries received from having tied his bicycle to the back of a bus.

If you have such a child there is little that you can do. Trying to change a child's behavior will only cause you to suffer from the Expectant Personality Disorder. Unfortunately, many parents attempt the "hold your breath until the child grows up" approach. However, such behavior only compounds the brain damage already caused from banging your head against the wall.

NEWROSES MAKERS
A well-known NEWrosis-producing politician.

NEWROSES MAKERS

In this section we would like to honor those who have contributed the most to the level of emotional disturbance in our society with a special "NEWroses ACHIEVEMENT AWARD."

NEWroses-Producing Politicians

NEWrotics, like all of us, need inspiration to help them along their way. The following words of wisdom from some of our greatest leaders have gone far towards that end:

"If each American had a shovel,
we could survive a limited nuclear war."

Secretary of Defense

"If you've seen one redwood tree,
you've seen them all."

James Watt

"A balanced budget in 1984."

Former actor R. Reagan

"Try to see it from the med-fly's point of view."

Former Governor Jerry Brown

NEWroses-Producing Geographic Locations

Where should an aspiring NEWrotic live? Here are the areas, which in the recent past have helped to make life especially interesting for their residents.

Love Canal

Three Mile Island

Mt. Saint Helens

Times Beach

NEWroses-Producing Movies

Jaws

Halloween

Psycho

Texas Chainsaw Massacre

Alien

These films have single-handedly ruined swimming, "trick-or-treating," showering, wood-chopping, and outer space for all of us.

NEWroses-Producing Diet and Exercise Programs

Richard Simmons Television Show: Makes you so happy to be fat you don't want to go on a diet.

Heavy Hands: A best seller which advises you to carry weights with you while you do things you already hate like jogging.

Life Extension: Before you take this book seriously, first take a long, hard look at the pictures of the authors.

I Love Beverly Hills Diet: Too rich.

Achievement Awards

There are certain outstanding individuals whose level of NEWroses is so impressive they must be singled out for recognition. Here are this season's winners:

Woody Allen: Most NEWrotic Neurotic.

George Steinbrenner/Billy Martin: Most NEWrotic Relationship.

Tootsie: Most NEWrotic Sex Symbol.

John DeLorean: Most NEWrotic Corporate Executive.